Secrets of the Sea

First U.S. edition 2017

Library of Congress Catalog Card Number pending
ISBN 978-0-7636-9839-3

17 18 19 20 21 22 LEO 10 9 8 7 6 5 4 3 2 1

Printed in Heshan, Guangdong, China

This book was typeset in Gabriela and ITC Goudy Sans.
The illustrations were done in mixed media.

BIG PICTURE PRESS
an imprint of
Candlewick Press
99 Dover Street
Somerville, Massachusetts 02144

www.candlewick.com

Secrets of the Sea

written by Kate Baker

illustrated by Eleanor Taylor

B P P

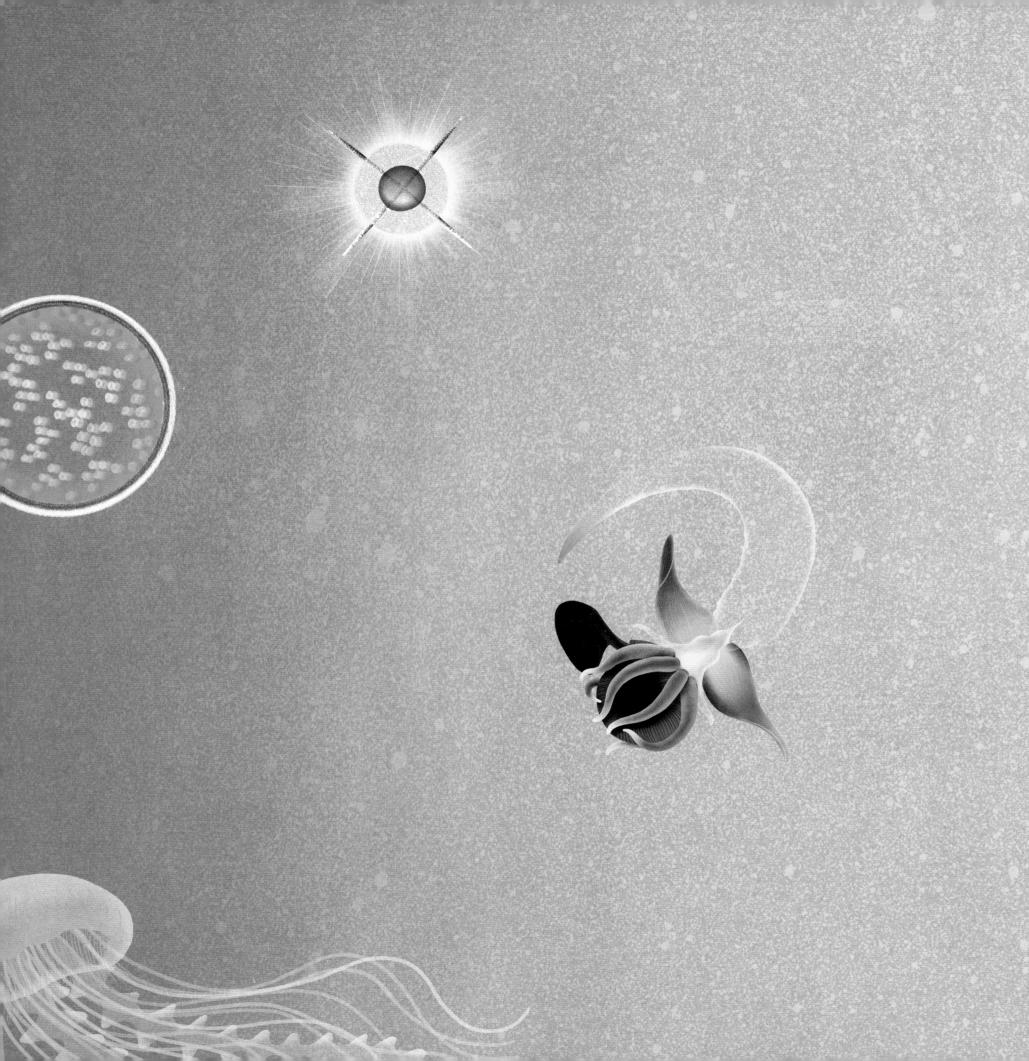

Contents

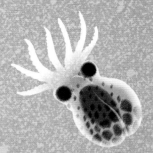

Introduction

The oceans are the place where all life on Earth began, yet they are one of the least understood places on the planet. From the sunlit shallows to the darkest depths, this book shines a light on a few of the extraordinary creatures that live beneath the waves. Some can change color, shape, or form in an instant, allowing them to "disappear" in plain sight. Others are so small that millions of them could fit in a single drop of water. Without them, life as we know it would not exist.

In the Shallows

From tide pools to tropical sandy shores,
the sun-drenched shallow waters that fringe
our planet's continents teem with life. Seaweed
and mollusks cling to the rocks, fish feed on
crustaceans, and sea anemones trap food with
their sticky tentacles. And at a microscopic level,
a bewildering array of minuscule creatures fights
for survival in this nutrient-rich ecosystem.

Common Blenny

| Latin name: *Lipophrys pholis* | Size: 6¼ inches/16 centimeters |
A small fish with a long, slender body

Blennies are small reclusive fish that can be found in such places as along the shores of the United Kingdom. The coloration and behaviors of some blennies have evolved to mimic those of other fish — helping them to either get a meal or avoid becoming one. Saber-toothed blennies look and act like cleaner wrasse, which feed on parasites of other fish. As an unsuspecting fish comes in for a cleaning, it gets chomped by a blenny instead.

Common blennies spend much of their time hidden in the crevices of tide pools, observing the world around them.

Their patterned bodies blend in well with nearby seaweed, limpets, rocks, and shells.

At high tide they emerge from their rocky hideaways to forage for food.

A common blenny, well camouflaged in a tide pool

Coconut Octopus

| LATIN NAME: *AMPHIOCTOPUS MARGINATUS* | BODY SIZE: 3 INCHES/8 CENTIMETERS, ARM LENGTH: 6 INCHES/15 CENTIMETERS |
A MEDIUM-SIZE CEPHALOPOD FOUND IN TROPICAL WATERS

Like other octopuses, the shape-shifting coconut octopus is a master of disguise, able to change color, form, and texture to blend in with its surroundings. But this clever creature has another, unique way of keeping itself safe from predators: it wraps its long arms, lined with rows of gripping suckers, around a half coconut shell or large seashell, then scampers with it across the ocean floor and uses it to make a nifty little hideout.

Octopuses are considered the most intelligent of all invertebrates and have an amazing ability to learn.

They have been known to climb aboard fishing boats and can unscrew jars and navigate mazes.

Since the only hard part of an octopus is its beak, it is able to squeeze into astonishingly small spaces.

A coconut octopus peering
out from a seashell

6

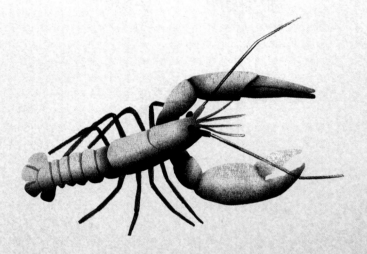

European Lobster

| LATIN NAME: *HOMARUS GAMMARUS* | SIZE: EGGS $1/16$ INCH/2 MILLIMETERS, ADULTS 16 INCHES/40 CENTIMETERS |
THESE LOBSTERS ARE LARGE CRUSTACEANS CLOSELY RELATED TO THE AMERICAN LOBSTER.

As summer approaches, female European lobsters return to the warmth of
the shallows to find a safe place to hatch their eggs. Each female may have as
many as 100,000 eggs nestled safely under her abdomen, each no bigger than
a pinhead. Once the eggs have hatched, the female lifts her tail and the tiny
larvae drift up to the surface, where they will feed on plankton. As they grow,
they molt, and with each molt, they gradually take on their adult form. Once
the transformation is complete, they sink to the ocean floor.

Only a small number of the
millions of eggs hatched
each summer will survive
the larval stage.

A lobster continues to
molt throughout its life
by splitting its shell-like
exoskeleton in two.

A newly molted lobster is
soft and vulnerable and
tries to stay hidden until
its shell hardens.

European lobster eggs as
seen under a microscope

Horseshoe Crab

| LATIN NAME: *LIMULUS POLYPHEMUS* | SIZE: EGGS $1/16$ INCH/2 MILLIMETERS, ADULTS 16 INCHES/40 CENTIMETERS |
DESPITE ITS NAME, THIS ANIMAL IS NOT A CRAB AT ALL BUT AN ARTHROPOD, LIKE SPIDERS AND SCORPIONS.

It is late spring. The tide is high and the full moon shines brightly on the sandy shoreline as an army of armored horseshoe crabs creeps up the beach. They have come here to breed. The females go up past the high-tide line and dig small nests in the mud or sand for their eggs. The eggs make a tempting treat for birds, reptiles, and fish. Those that survive return to the ocean after hatching and burrow into the seafloor. There they molt and grow before venturing into deeper waters.

A female can lay hundreds of thousands of eggs over the course of several nights.

Horseshoe crabs have ten eyes, distributed around their body. Some of the eyes are merely light sensors but can also detect movement.

Horseshoe crabs today look very similar to the horseshoe crabs that crept along the shorelines 350 million years ago.

Horseshoe crab egg as seen under a microscope

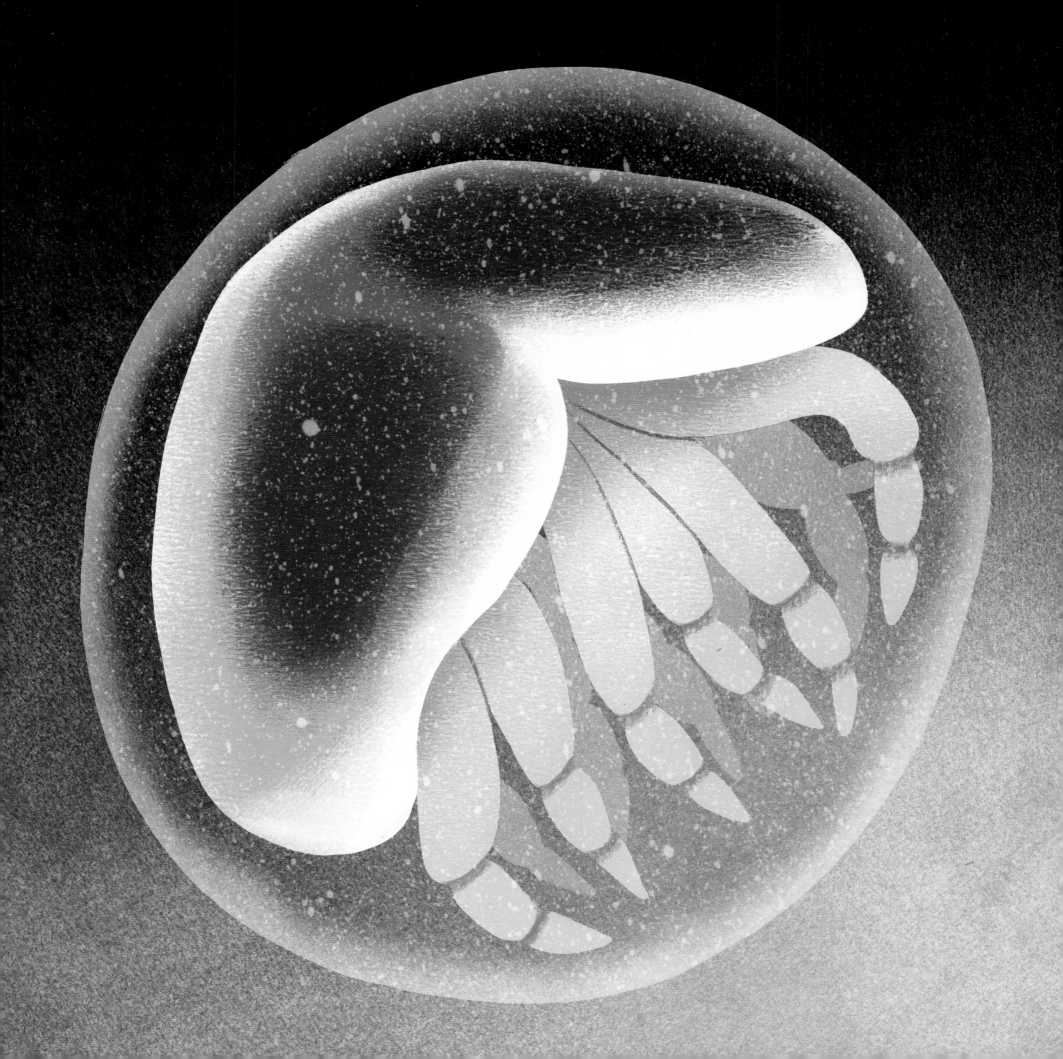

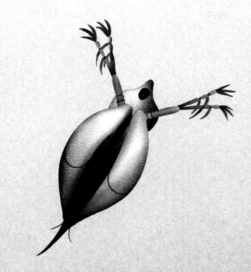

Daphnia

| LATIN NAME: *DAPHNIA MAGNA* | SIZE: $1/8$ INCH/3 MILLIMETERS |
A TINY CRUSTACEAN WITH FLAT LEAF-LIKE LEGS

These creatures, sometimes called water fleas, are too small to be seen in detail with the naked eye, but when viewed under a microscope, they soon reveal their secrets. Their bodies are transparent, so their beating heart is visible, as is the course of the blood cells around their body. Females have brood chambers on their backs, which protect their minuscule eggs.

Though commonly referred to as water fleas, daphnia are crustaceans and are more closely related to crabs.

Daphnia move through the water in a jerky, hopping motion, using their antennae.

Most species of daphnia feed on bacteria and very small algae via a method called filter feeding, which is also how some whales eat.

A female daphnia, under a microscope, with eggs in her brood chamber

Sea Sparkle

| Latin name: *Noctiluca scintillans* | Size: 0.5 millimeter |
A single-celled organism that can glow blue at night

Single-celled organisms known as sea sparkle float in coastal waters in swarms of millions. They are bioluminescent, meaning they can emit light. They may do so to startle and scare away predators. As fish and other creatures swim through the water, they disturb the sea sparkle, which then glow a vivid fluorescent blue. During a population increase, called a bloom, they tend to appear red or pink.

Sea sparkle is technically not an animal. It's an organism called a dinoflagellate.

At night, fishermen sometimes use the bright light from the sea sparkle to help them see fish in the darkness.

Sea sparkle is also known as sea ghost. Its scientific name translates as "twinkling night light."

Sea sparkle as seen under a microscope

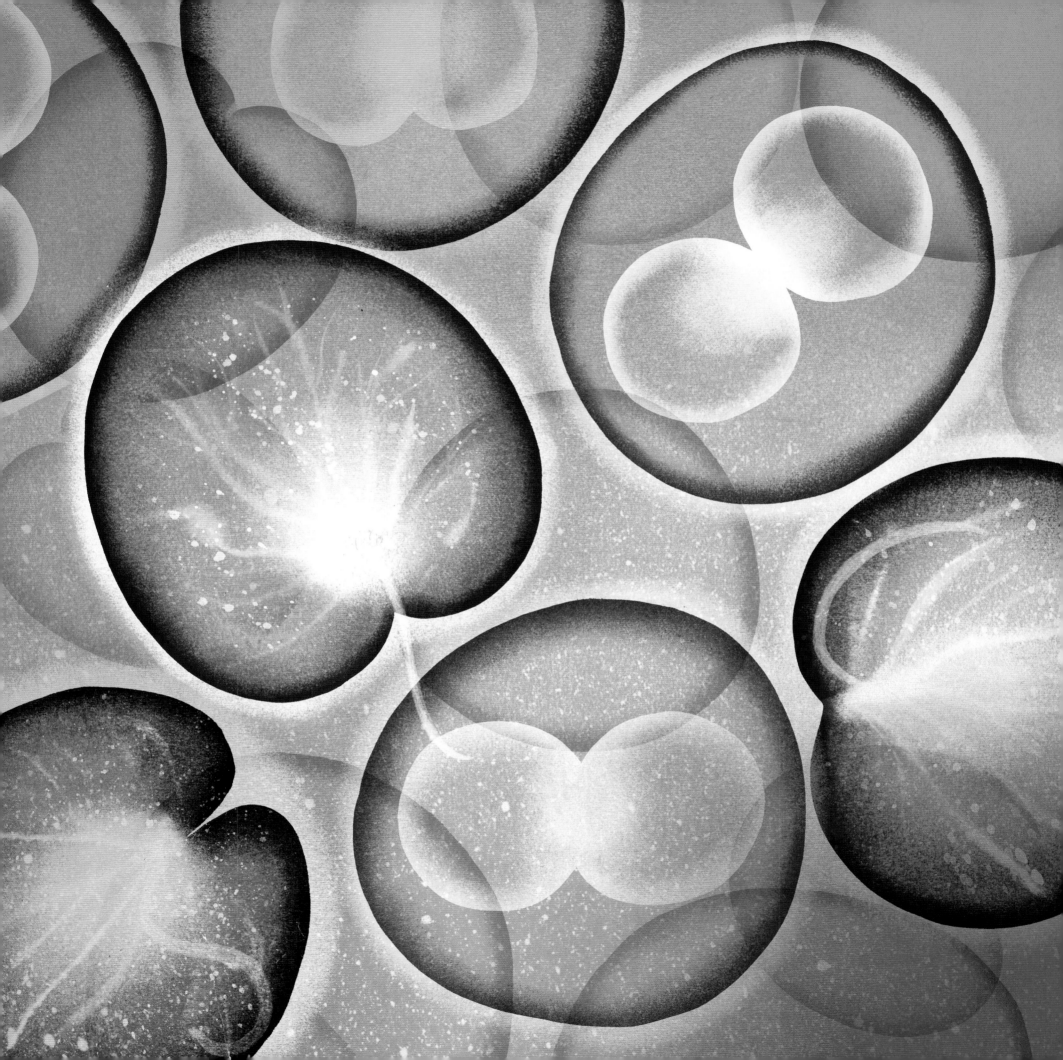

Bryozoa

| Size: 0.5–1 millimeter |

MILLIONS OF THESE TINY ORGANISMS MIGHT LIVE IN ONE COLONY.

Each individual is known as a zooid and lives in its own hard calcareous "house" less than 1 millimeter long.

Larval bryozoans come in many different forms. The most common is triangular with a tuft of hairlike cilia at the top. A larva swims through the water before settling on a frond of seaweed.

Once settled, the larva cements itself firmly to the surface of the seaweed and begins changing into its adult form. The rest of the colony will grow from this first individual zooid.

Using their circular ring of feeding tentacles, or lophophores, bryozoans sieve tiny particles of food from the water.

In increasing order of magnification:
Left: A colony of bryozoans on a seaweed frond
Center: A close-up of a colony of bryozoans on a seaweed frond
Right: A single bryozoan as seen under a microscope

Common Sea Star

| LATIN NAME: *ASTERIAS RUBENS* | SIZE: 6 INCHES/15 CENTIMETERS |
SEA STARS BELONG TO A GROUP CALLED ECHINODERMS, A TERM MEANING "SPINY-SKINNED."

The larval form of the common sea star looks very unlike its adult self. The reproductive process begins when females release millions of eggs, which are fertilized externally, into the water. A female sea star can produce as many as 2.5 million eggs at a time. After fertilization, an egg develops into a hollow ball covered with tiny, hairlike structures and drifts freely in the sea.

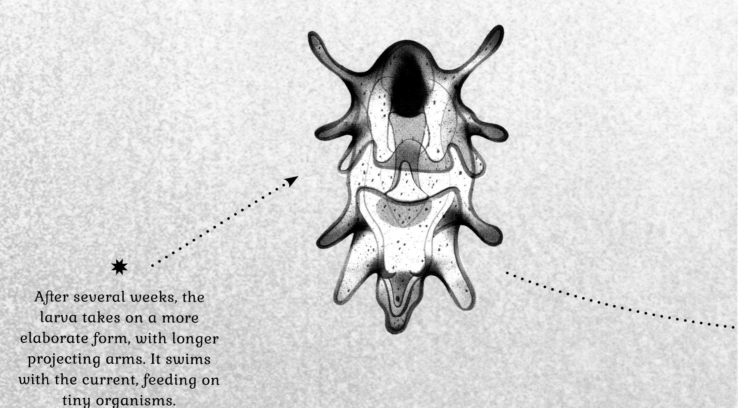

After several weeks, the larva takes on a more elaborate form, with longer projecting arms. It swims with the current, feeding on tiny organisms.

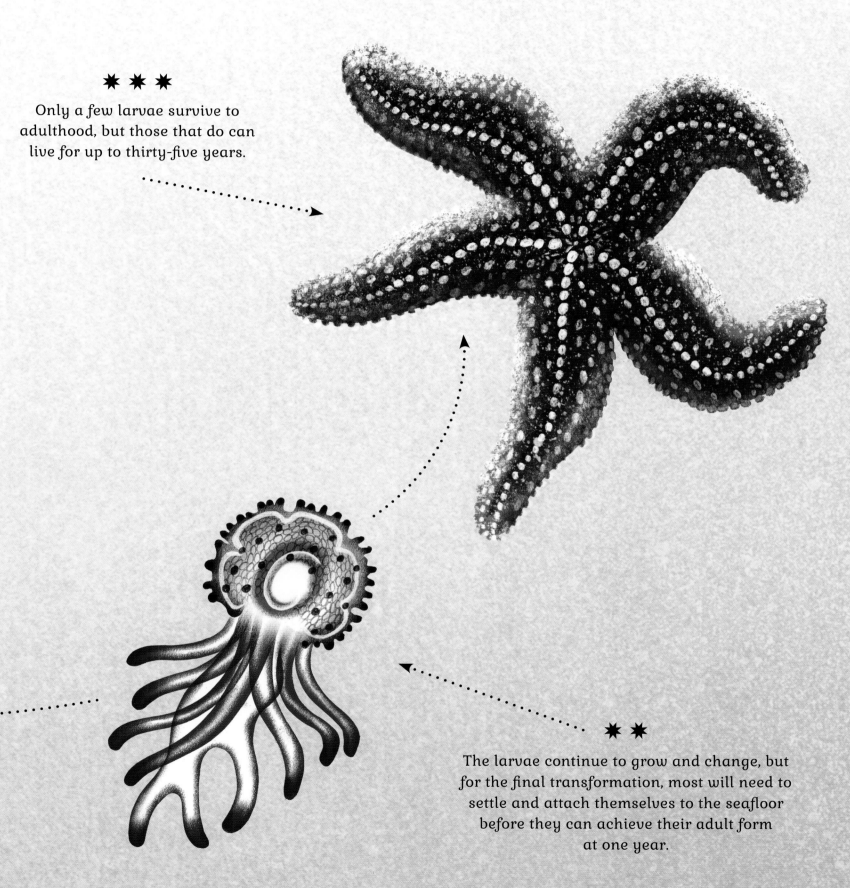

★ ★ ★

Only a few larvae survive to adulthood, but those that do can live for up to thirty-five years.

★ ★

The larvae continue to grow and change, but for the final transformation, most will need to settle and attach themselves to the seafloor before they can achieve their adult form at one year.

Left and above: Microscopic views of sea star larvae at different stages of growth

Forests of the Sea

Stretching along temperate coasts, lush forests of giant kelp thrive in the summer sunshine. These vast seaweed towers — some as tall as 175 feet/53 meters — can grow by 2 feet/60 centimeters each day. Many organisms make their homes here. Sea lions and sea otters pirouette above the sand, orange Garibaldi fish seek shelter in the canopy, and thousands of brittle stars and flower-like anemones carpet the forest floor. Meanwhile, young sea snails graze on the kelp blades as great armies of purple sea urchins eat away at the tangled roots.

Giant Kelp

| LATIN NAME: *MACROCYSTIS PYRIFERA* | HEIGHT: 100 FEET/30 METERS |
THE LARGEST SPECIES OF KELP, A COMPLEX FORM OF BROWN ALGAE

Giant kelp grows in thick forests that create one of the most productive
and dynamic ecosystems on Earth. Each day hundreds of ocean creatures use the forest as
a nursery for their young, for shelter during storms, and as a vital source of food. The kelp
itself is made of tough stems, or stipes, that are flexible enough to sway in the strong ocean
current. The kelp is able to obtain all the nutrients it needs directly from the water.

Kelp isn't a plant, so it doesn't have roots. It is anchored to the seafloor by a spaghetti-like structure called a holdfast.

Just one holdfast can be home to hundreds of animal species, including brittle stars, kelp crabs, and baby octopuses.

At the base of each leafy frond is an air bladder, a balloon-like bubble that holds the kelp upright.

Close-up view of a kelp blade

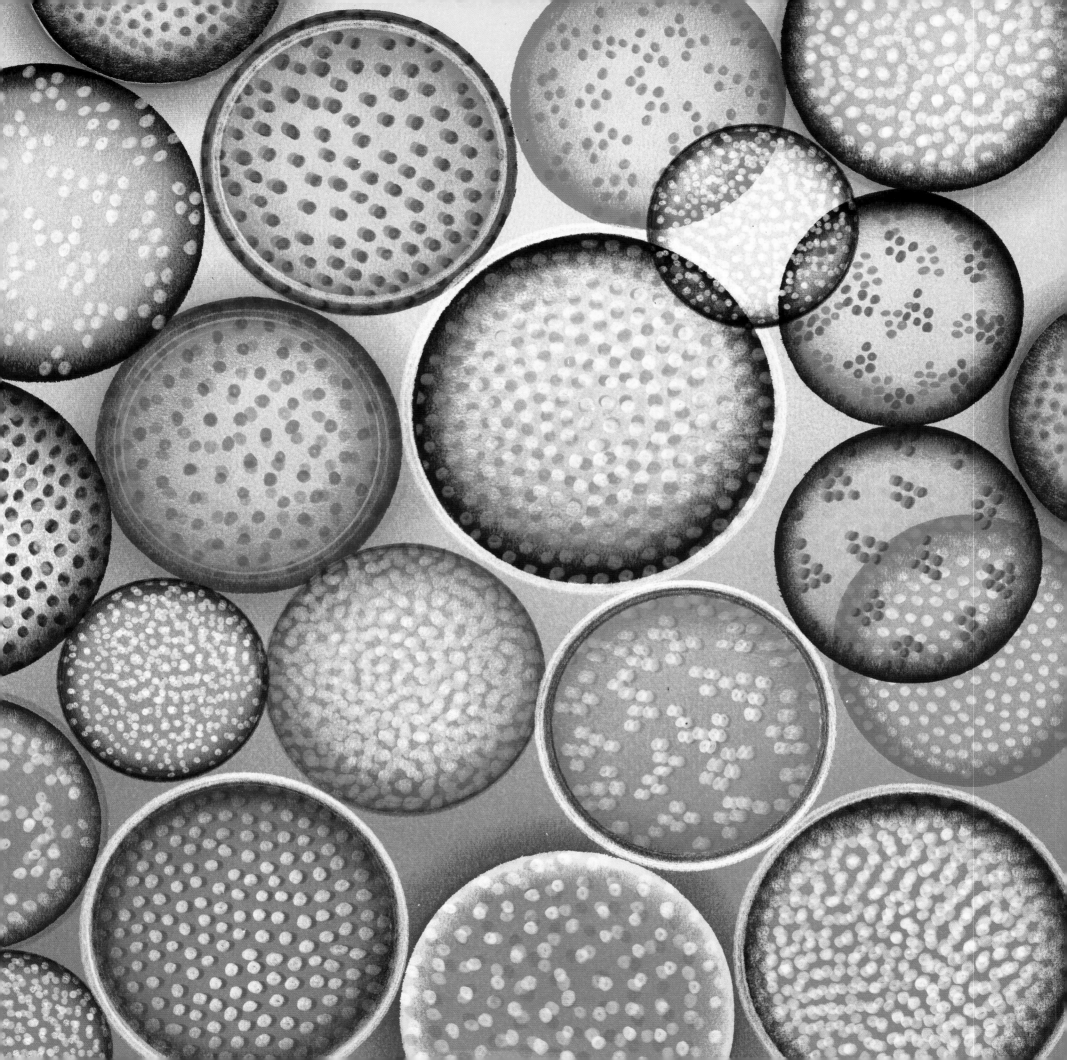

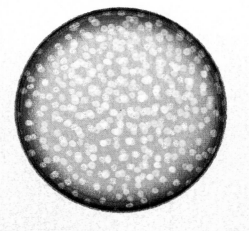

Cyanobacteria

| Size: 0.5–50 micrometers |

A primitive photosynthesizing bacteria so small you could fit a thousand on a pinhead

More than three and a half billion years ago, a new life-form evolved on Earth: cyanobacteria. These primitive bacteria are sometimes known as blue-green algae, but that term is inaccurate since they are bacteria rather than algae. Cyanobacteria were the first organisms to undergo photosynthesis — taking in energy from the sun, converting it into food to fuel their cells' needs, and releasing oxygen as a by-product. This helped to turn Earth's atmosphere into one rich in oxygen, enabling the evolution of air-breathing creatures — like us!

Cyanobacteria fossils are among the oldest fossils we've found.

Together with algae, cyanobacteria form a vital part of the marine food web and produce much of the air we breathe.

Cyanobacteria are microscopic but often grow in colonies that are large enough to see.

Cyanobacteria as seen under a microscope

Hooded Nudibranch

| LATIN NAME: *MELIBE LEONINA* | SIZE: UP TO 7 INCHES/17.5 CENTIMETERS LONG, 1 INCH/3 CENTIMETERS WIDE |
A PREDATORY SEA SLUG, ALSO CALLED THE LION'S MANE NUDIBRANCH

This otherworldly creature can be found attached to the holdfasts of kelp all along the west coast of North America, swimming from frond to frond, feeding, mating, and laying its eggs. It hunts by throwing out its large hood, which is fringed with sensory tentacles, and then snapping the hood shut to capture its prey. The prey is then forced into the nudibranch's mouth.

As a defense mechanism, this creature secretes a substance that some people report smells sweet, like fruit.

The paddle-like plates that line its back are its gills. These can detach if the nudibranch is threatened.

Eggs are laid in long, wide yellow or creamy-colored ribbons and are attached to kelp and eelgrass.

Close-up view of a hooded nudibranch

26

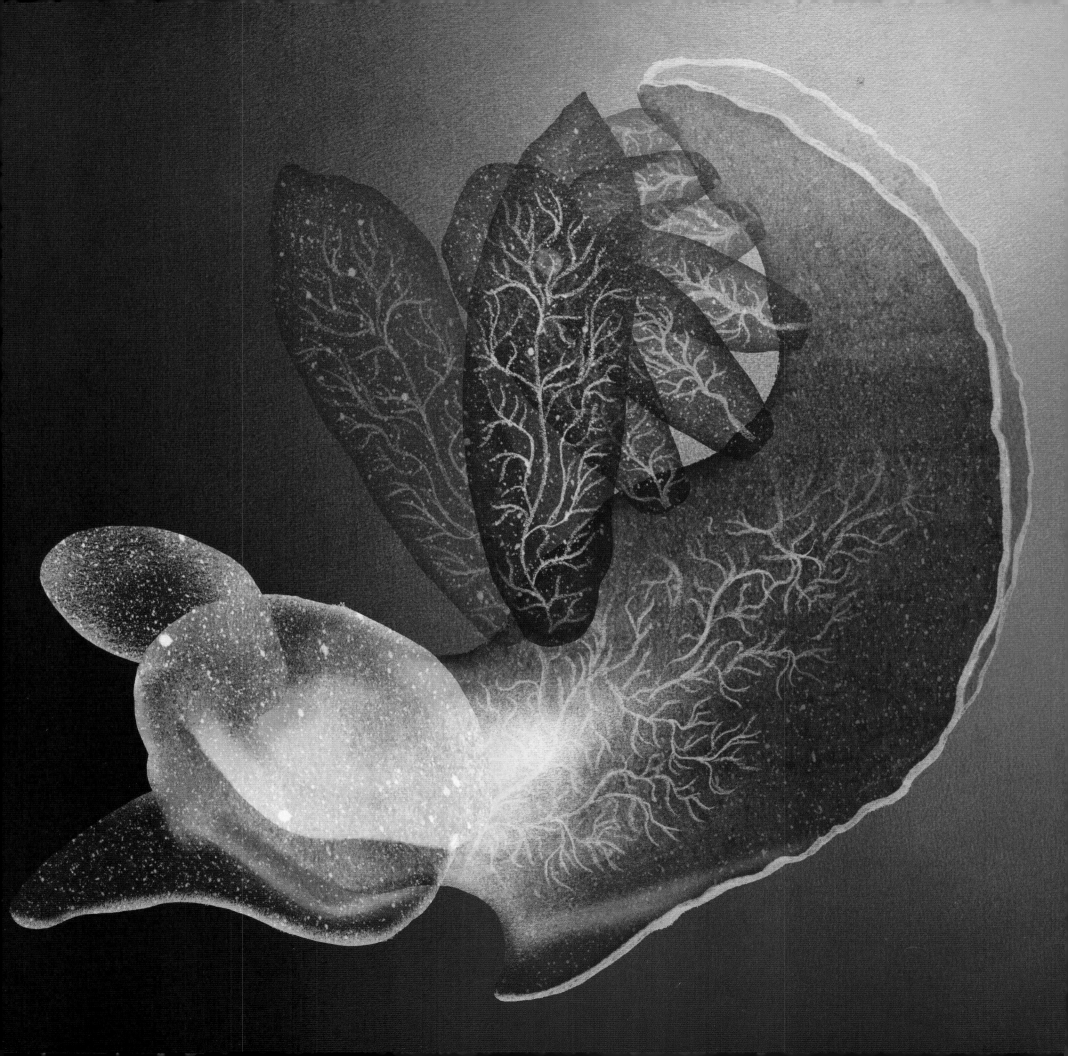

Fish Gills

MOST FISH RELY ON THIS RESPIRATORY ORGAN, THOUGH THE NUMBER OF GILLS VARIES.

When viewed up close, fish gills resemble the branches of a beautiful sea plant. These extraordinary organs enable a fish to breathe and work in much the same way as lungs do — they extract oxygen from the environment and expel carbon dioxide. The arrangement of cells seen here, branch-like structures dividing into ever-smaller branches, creates a large surface area to help the fish maximize the absorption of oxygen from the water.

As a fish swims, it pulls oxygenated water through its mouth and passes it across its gills, which are rich in blood.

The oxygen is absorbed into the fish's bloodstream, and its heart pumps the blood around its body.

At the same time, waste carbon dioxide in the blood seeps back through the gills and into the water.

Fish gills as seen under a microscope

Purple Sea Urchin

| LATIN NAME: *STRONGYLOCENTROTUS PURPURATUS* | SIZE: 2 INCHES/5 CENTIMETERS ACROSS |
A SMALL, SPINY ANIMAL WITH A MOUTH ON THE UNDERSIDE OF ITS BODY

This strange, spiky creature moves slowly across the kelp-forest floors of the eastern Pacific Ocean. Despite their impressive armor, urchins are a popular meal for sea otters, fish, crabs, and seabirds. Without such predators to help control numbers, hordes of hungry sea urchins can devastate a giant kelp forest. Over time, the area would become a barren underwater desert.

The round shell of an urchin is called a test and is covered with pincers, tube feet, and spines.

The urchin's spines are razor-sharp and move on ball-and-socket joints. If broken off, they can regenerate.

Most urchins have five self-sharpening teeth that they use to feast on the algae at the base of the kelp's holdfasts.

Close-up view of a purple sea urchin

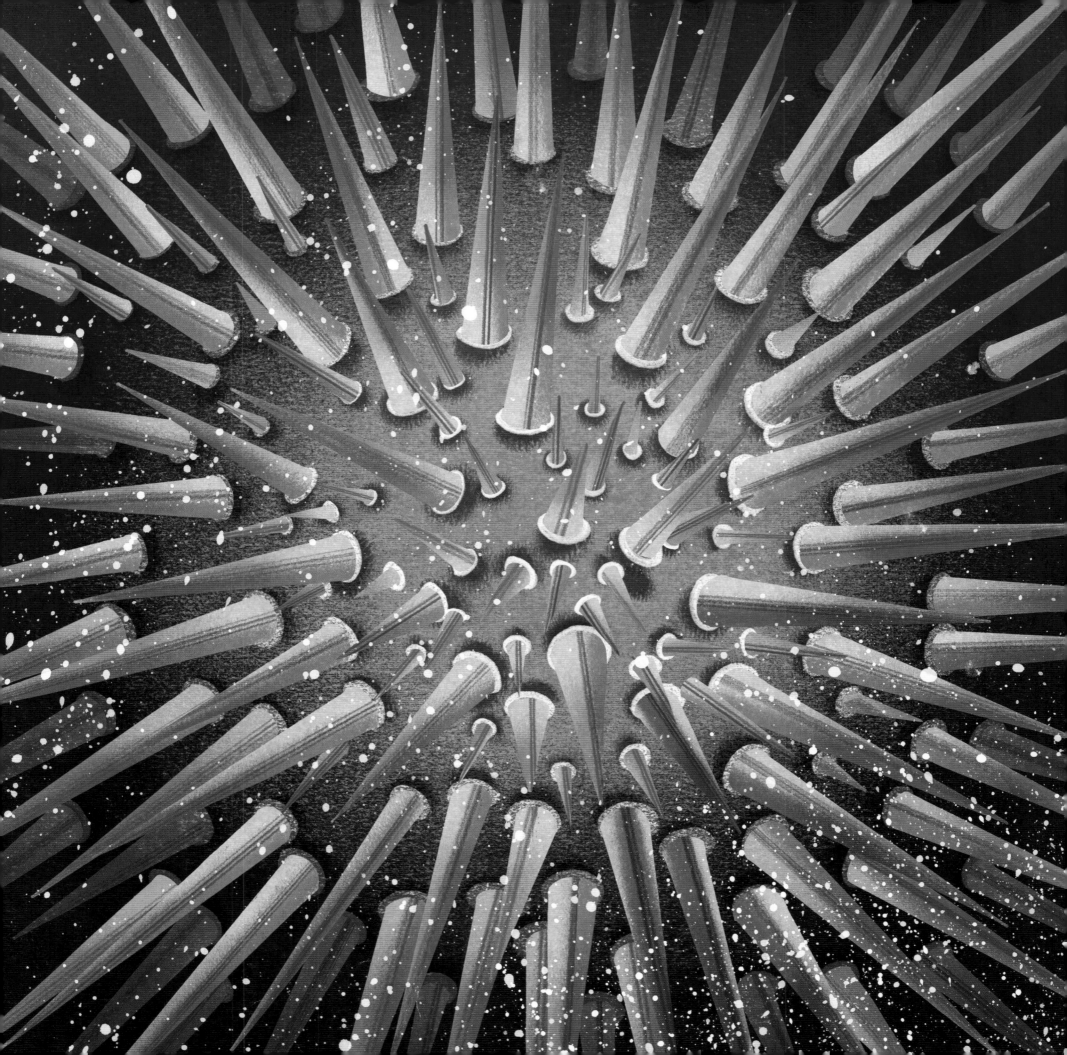

Diatoms

| Size: 2–500 micrometers |

Microscopic, single-celled algae that live suspended near the ocean's surface

These microscopic algae are one of the most important organisms in the world's oceans. Largely photosynthetic, they convert sunlight into food and then release oxygen. This process accounts for a large percentage of the oxygen in the atmosphere. Diatoms are also an important source of food for all kinds of microorganisms and larger animals, including shrimp, snails, jellies, and whales.

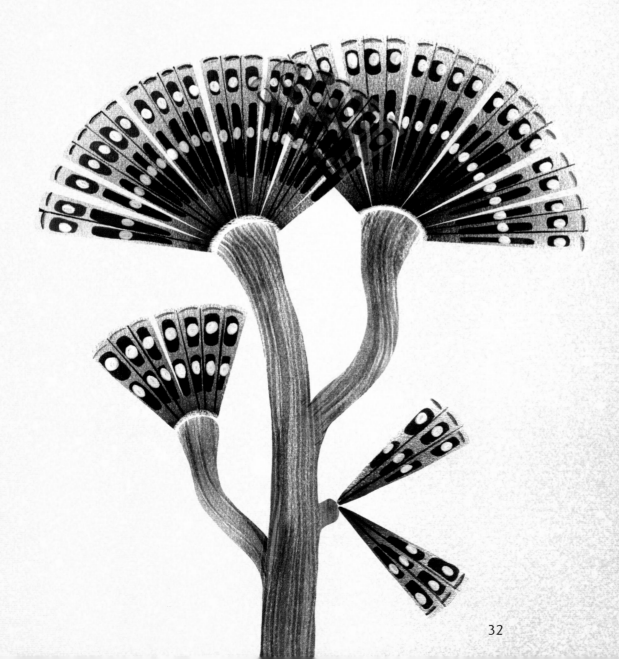

Every day, millions of minuscule zooplankton rise from the depths to dine on diatoms.

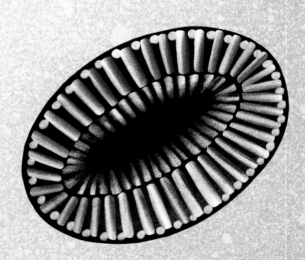

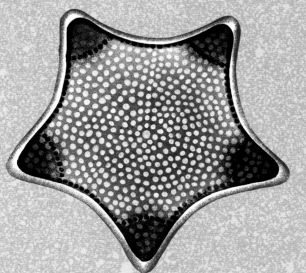

Diatoms are so small that hundreds of them could fit on the head of a pin, but when congregated in vast blooms, they are visible from outer space.

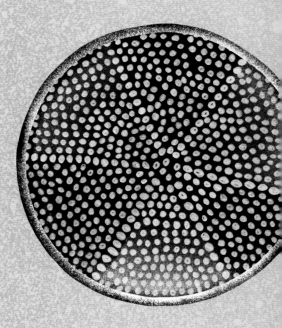

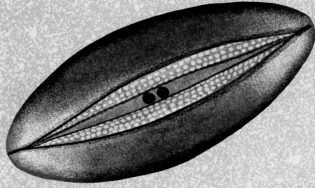

Diatoms are enclosed within a cell wall, or frustule, which is made of silica and has an ornate, intricate structure.

Diatoms live individually or in groups, forming zigzags, chains, or spirals.

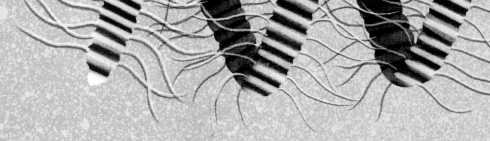

Coral Gardens

In the clear sunlit waters of tropical and subtropical seas, we find one of the natural world's most precious treasures: the coral reef. These vital habitats for an incredible array of ocean life are built incrementally over centuries by minuscule colonial animals called polyps. Coral reefs are home to almost a quarter of all fish on our planet. The creatures found here are vividly colored and strikingly diverse, and each plays its own special role in the reef.

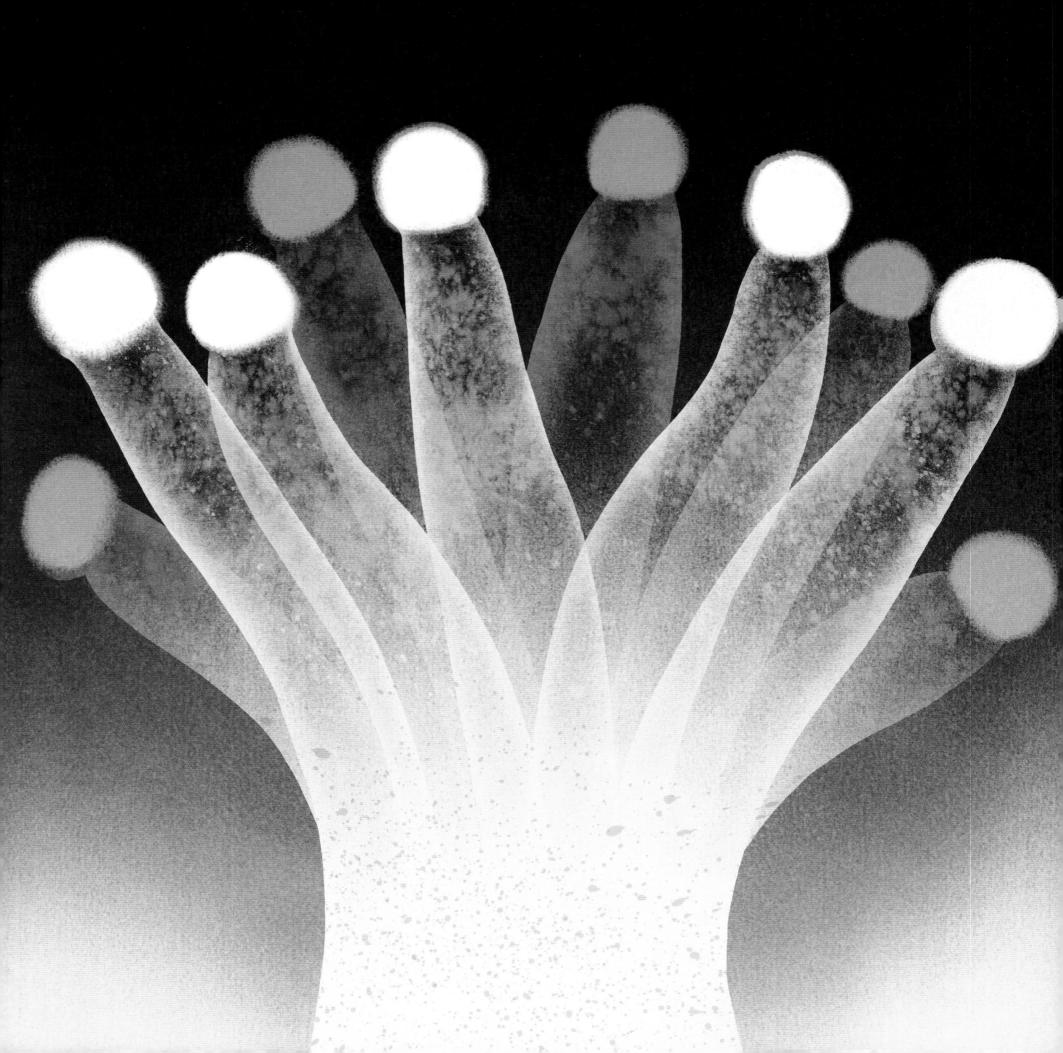

Coral Polyp

| SIZE: 1/4 INCH–12 INCHES/6 MILLIMETERS–30 CENTIMETERS |
A SOFT-BODIED INVERTEBRATE WITH A MOUTH ENCIRCLED BY TENTACLES

Although they look like ornate gardens filled with exotic plants, coral reefs are actually the work of tiny animals called polyps. Reefs are formed when a free-swimming coral larva attaches itself to a rock on the seafloor. The polyp then clones itself to create vast colonies, made up of thousands of individuals. By day, the polyps retreat into their stony skeletons, soaking up the sun's rays. At night, their buds open like flowers and they extend their stinging tentacles to snare drifting plankton.

At the base of the polyp is a hard limestone skeleton, which protects the polyp and forms the structure of the reef.

As colonies grow over hundreds and thousands of years, they join with other colonies and become reefs.

Some reefs are so enormous they can be seen from space. Some began growing 50 million years ago.

Close-up view of a coral polyp

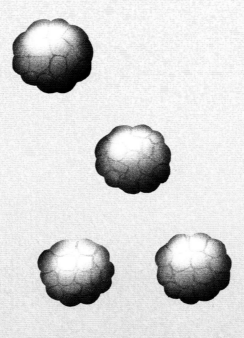

Galaxy Coral

| LATIN NAME: *GALAXEA FASCICULARIS* | SIZE: POLYPS $3/8$ INCH/9 MILLIMETERS ACROSS |
SOME SPECIES OF CORAL REPRODUCE IN LARGE, SYNCHRONIZED EVENTS CALLED SPAWNING.

The sun has set, the moon is rising, and the reef is ready to put on one of
nature's most extraordinary spectacles: a mass coral spawning event.
Trillions of reproductive cells from many different colonies and species of
coral are simultaneously released. They unite to form free-swimming larvae.
Those that survive drift for days before settling on the ocean floor, where
they clone themselves to create whole new colonies.

The timing of these events is
still a mystery, but scientists
theorize that sea temperature
and the phase of the moon both
play a part.

Spawning coral create what
looks like an underwater
pink snowstorm.

Coral larvae are attracted
to light and will sometimes
stay near the water's surface
for weeks.

Close-up view of galaxy
coral spawning

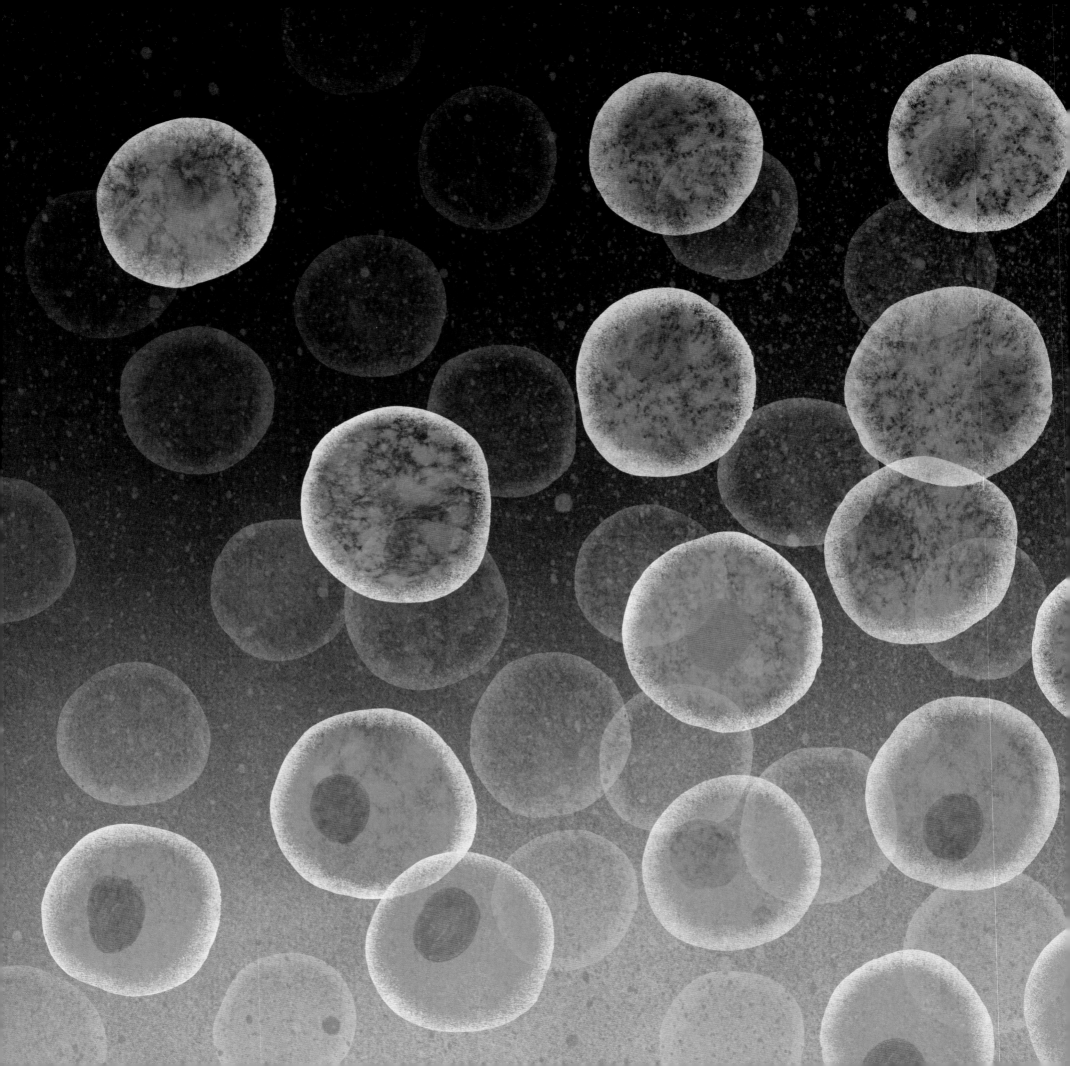

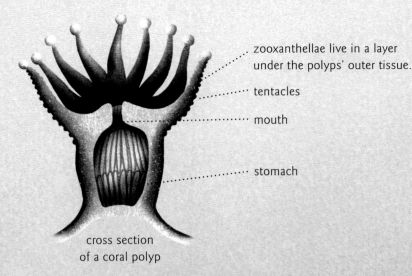

zooxanthellae live in a layer
under the polyps' outer tissue.

tentacles

mouth

stomach

cross section
of a coral polyp

Zooxanthellae

| SIZE: 5 MICROMETERS |

THESE SINGLE-CELLED PHOTOSYNTHETIC ALGAE LIVE INSIDE A CORAL POLYP.

The amazing biodiversity of coral reefs is possible because of the symbiotic relationship between corals and their zooxanthellae. Part plant, part animal, these microscopic wonders, which live inside the polyps, turn sunlight into energy and food. In return, the coral gives the zooxanthellae nutrients and a safe place to live. Together they turn barren seas into rich gardens.

Coral polyps are actually translucent animals. Many reefs get their dazzling hues from the colors of the zooxanthellae.

When the zooxanthellae are stressed by conditions such as high temperatures, they will die or leave their host.

Without the zooxanthellae, the coral loses its main source of food. It bleaches and eventually dies.

Zooxanthellae as seen under
a microscope

Pygmy Sea Horse

| LATIN NAME: *HIPPOCAMPUS BARGIBANTI* | SIZE: ³/4 INCH/2 CENTIMETERS |
SEA HORSES ARE SMALL FISH WITH A PREHENSILE TAIL.

On the edge of the reef around Australia, a soft coral called a gorgonian
sea fan stretches its tree-like branches toward the sunlight. Tucked inside,
clinging tightly to the coral with its tail, is the pygmy sea horse, one of the
smallest vertebrates in the world. A pygmy sea horse will live out almost its
entire adult life hidden in the safety of the sea fan.

Each morning, courting sea
horse couples perform a
graceful dance, mirroring
each other's movements as
they sway on the current.

The calcified bumps on
the sea horse's skin match
the color and shape of
the sea fan's polyps — the
perfect camouflage.

As with all sea horses,
the male carries eggs
in a brood pouch on his
body from which the live
young emerge.

Pygmy sea horses nestled
in a gorgonian sea fan

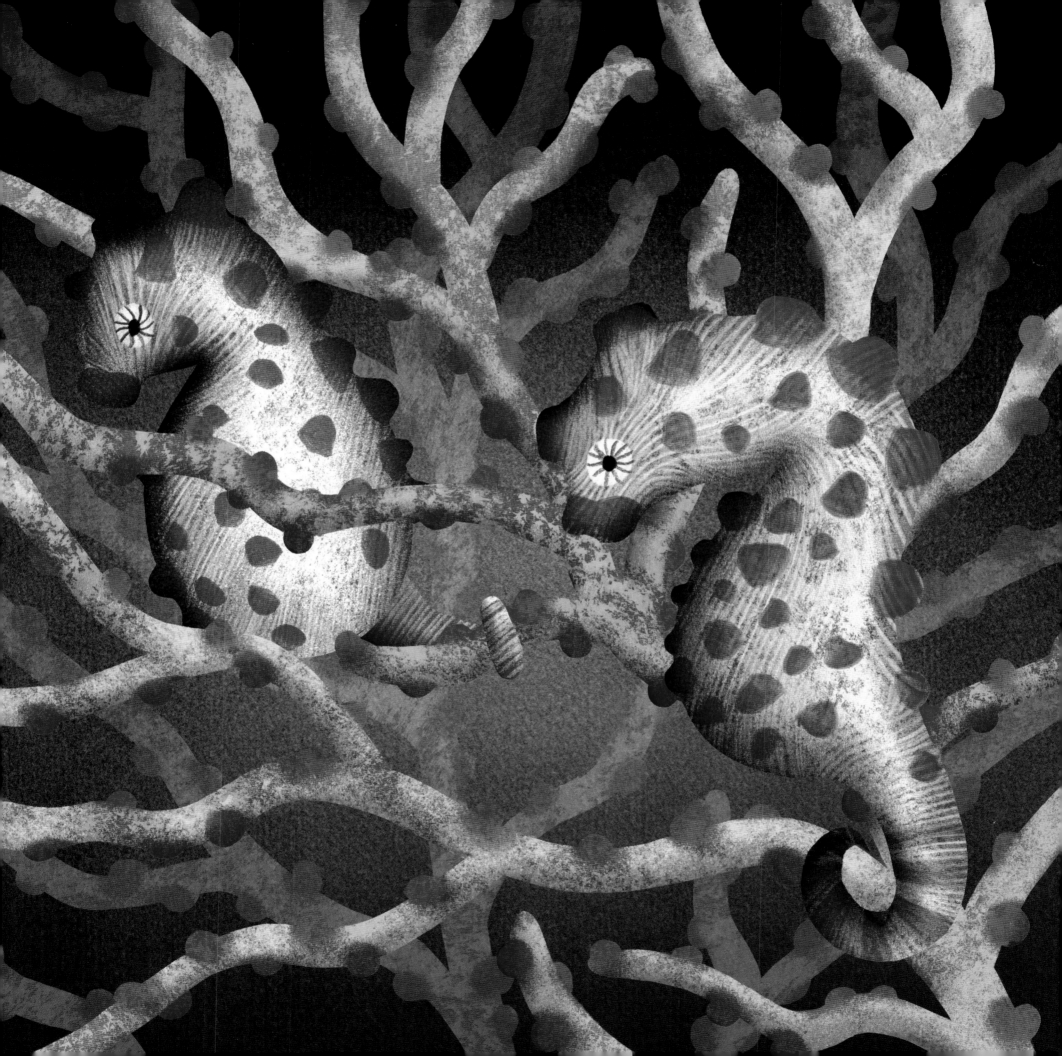

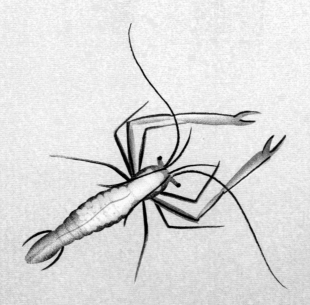

Bubble Coral Shrimp

| Latin name: *Vir philippinensis* | Size: $3/4$ inch/2 centimeters |
A small crustacean with red antennae and thin purple markings on its legs

Bubble coral is topped with distinctive grape-size, water-filled bubbles, which retract at night so its feeding tentacles can emerge to gather prey. Much harder to spot is the bubble coral shrimp, one of the reef's most elusive inhabitants, nestled within the folds of bubble coral in the Western Pacific and in the Indian Ocean. With its tiny, translucent body and delicate legs, it is almost invisible to the naked eye.

Shrimp are incredibly adaptable. There are more than two thousand different species, found in environments from the tropics to the poles.

Pistol shrimp stun their prey by snapping their claws together to create a deafening *crack*.

Banded coral shrimp clean the scales of coral fish as the fish swim backward through the shrimp's pincers.

A bubble shrimp hiding on bubble coral

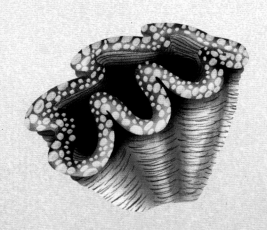

Giant Clam

| LATIN NAME: *TRIDACNA GIGAS* | SIZE: 4 FEET/1.2 METERS |
THESE MOLLUSKS LIVE IN THE SOUTH PACIFIC AND INDIAN OCEANS.

Tales have long been told of colossal man-eating clams, but in truth, the giant clam is one of the ocean's gentlest creatures. It hosts billions of algae in the safety of its tissues and, in turn, takes advantage of the sugar and protein the algae produce. The clam's "lips," which extrude from its dull outer shell, are called its mantle and are vividly colored in blues, greens, yellows, pinks, or browns. Giant clams can live for more than a hundred years and weigh more than 440 pounds/200 kilograms.

Each clam has its own unique colors and patterns, so no two clams are ever the same.

There are hundreds of tiny dark spots lining the clam's mantle. These are its eyes.

The clam's hard undulating shell provides a refuge for barnacles, sponges, and newborn fish.

Close-up view of a giant clam's mantle

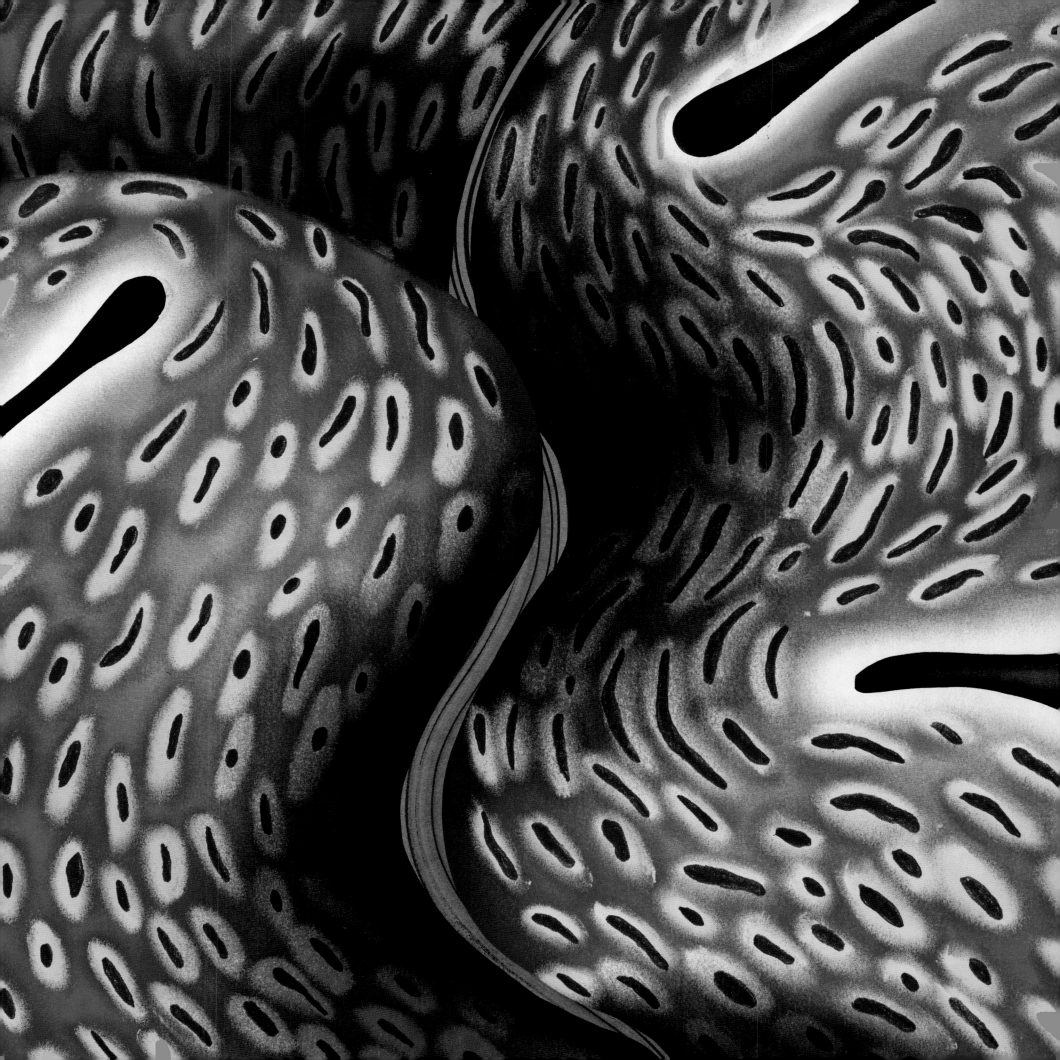

Queen Parrotfish

| LATIN NAME: *SCARUS VETULA* | SIZE: 15 INCHES/40 CENTIMETERS |
NUMEROUS TEETH ON THE SURFACE OF THIS FISH'S JAWBONE FORM A BEAK LIKE A PARROT'S.

Among coral reefs' colorful marvels is the iridescent queen parrotfish. Its exquisite scales are smooth and overlap to form a flexible protective skin. In some species, this jewel-like armor is strong enough to stop a spear. All parrotfish hatch as female. They can switch their sex at various points, depending on the population's needs. This is called sequential hermaphroditism.

Schools of parrotfish graze on dead coral in search of the algae that live inside.

The fish excrete the corals' stony skeletons as clouds of fine sediment, which helps to form white sand beaches.

Herbivores like the parrotfish help to prevent the reef from becoming choked by algae.

Close-up view of a queen parrotfish's scales

Zooplankton

| SIZE: 2 MICROMETERS–20 CENTIMETERS/8 INCHES |
ANIMALS THAT DRIFT IN THE OCEAN AND OTHER BODIES OF WATER

At night, water surrounding the coral reef fills with clouds of zooplankton that drift on the currents, feasting on planktonic plants. The zooplankton are eaten by marine animals of all sizes — from coral polyps, barnacles, and sea squirts to fish and whales. Some zooplankton, like diatoms and krill, are permanent zooplankton, and some are the larvae of larger animals like sea urchins and are classified as temporary zooplankton.

Copepod

Typically just 1–2 millimeters long, this tear-shaped crustacean is one of the most abundant species in the planktonic soup. Using their antennae and appendages like paddles, they glide, dart, and jump through the water.

A copepod's hairlike setae are used to collect food particles.

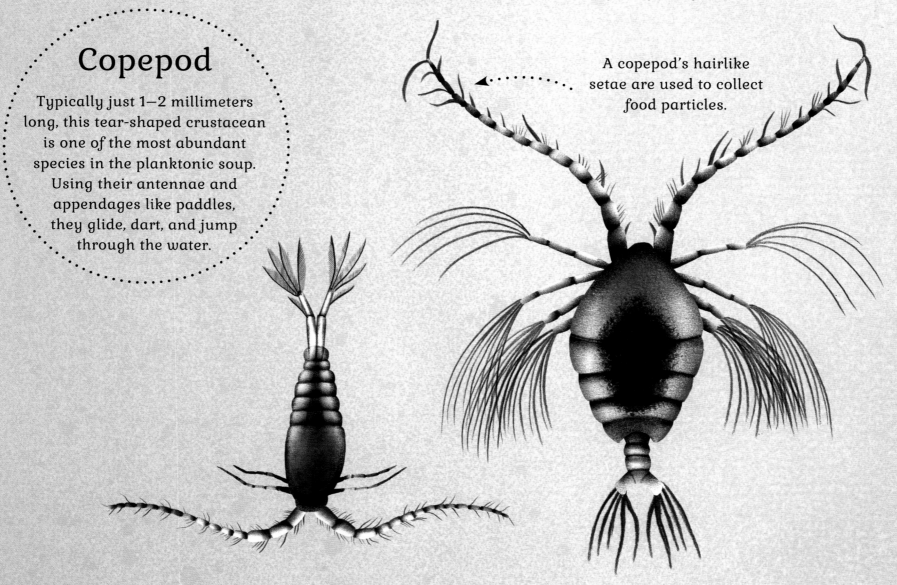

Crab larvae

The first larval stage of a crab, called a zoea, is barely the size of a grain of rice. The zoea bears little resemblance to the adult crab.

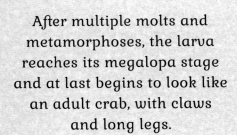

After multiple molts and metamorphoses, the larva reaches its megalopa stage and at last begins to look like an adult crab, with claws and long legs.

Copepods and crab larvae as seen under a microscope

Foraminifera

| SIZE: 1 MILLIMETER–8 INCHES/20 CENTIMETERS |
SINGLE-CELLED SHELLED ORGANISMS, SOMETIMES CALLED FORAMS

On the sandy floor of the reef are millions of foraminifera. Some float freely in the water, but most live on or in sand, mud, rocks, and plants. Most species are so small that they can only be seen through the lens of a microscope. As they die, their skeletons rain down on the seafloor and are preserved as fossils in the sediment below.

Foraminifera as seen under a microscope

Some foraminifera have internal shells known as tests.

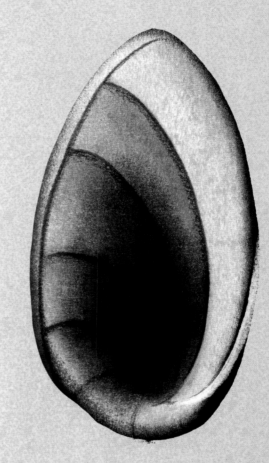

Over the ages, foraminifera-packed sediments on the seafloor have compacted, then risen up to form chalk cliffs. Many of the world's great sites, from the pink sands of Bermuda to the pyramids of Egypt, are filled with these microfossils.

These ancient forms first appeared on Earth 500–540 million years ago. By studying them, scientists are able to determine the health of the oceans and how global temperatures may have changed in the past.

The Wide, Wide Blue

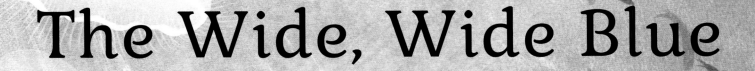

Away from the shorelines in deeper open waters are
organisms that live out their entire existence without
touching the shore, the seafloor, or the water's surface.
It is in these open waters that giants gather. Shoals
of barracuda and marlin glide like submarines on the
moving currents, and blue whales — the largest animals
on Earth — make epic voyages to their Arctic and
Antarctic feeding grounds. The waters near the surface,
bathed in light, are the most populated with ocean life.

Left: A blue dragon feasting on a man-of-war
Right: The Portuguese man-of-war

The Blue Dragon and the Man-of-War

| BLUE DRAGON | LATIN NAME: *GLAUCUS ATLANTICUS* |
| SIZE: 1 INCH/3 CENTIMETERS |
| PORTUGUESE MAN-OF-WAR | LATIN NAME: *PHYSALIA PHYSALIS* |
| SIZE: BODY 12 INCHES/30 CENTIMETERS, TENTACLES UP TO 165 FEET/50 METERS LONG |

The infamously dangerous tentacles of the Portuguese man-of-war are covered in lethal stinging cells, but the extraordinary, tiny blue dragon has an incredible relationship with the deadly creature. It is immune to the man-of-war's toxins and, in fact, stores them within its finger-like branches. When concentrated in the smaller blue dragon, the man-of-war's venom becomes even more powerful, making it deadly to touch.

Also known as a sea swallow or blue angel, the blue dragon is in fact a type of sea slug.

Often mistaken for a jelly, the man-of-war is a siphonophore, a whole colony of tiny organisms.

The Portuguese man-of-war gets its name from its gas-filled bladder, which resembles an old warship at full sail.

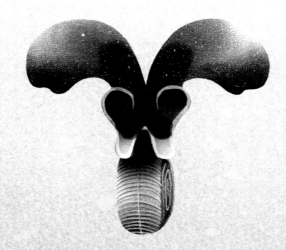

Sea Butterfly

| LATIN NAME: *LIMACINA HELICINA* | SIZE: $^1/_{16}$ INCH/2 MILLIMETERS |
A SMALL BUTTERFLY-LIKE MARINE SNAIL CRUCIAL TO THE OCEAN'S ECOSYSTEM

This strangely beautiful aquatic snail, found from the tropics to the poles, uses its heart-shaped muscular foot as a pair of "wings," soaring through the water like a tiny butterfly in flight. With a glassy shell and gelatinous body, the sea butterfly is extremely fragile and is easy prey for larger sea snails, fish, seabirds, and whales, and is sometimes called the potato chip of the sea.

The sea butterfly moves by clapping its wings behind it and then flinging them apart to propel itself forward.

It catches its prey, phytoplankton and small zooplankton, by producing a web of sticky mucus.

Similar to the shells of its terrestrial relatives, land snails, a sea butterfly's coiled shell is made of calcium carbonate.

A sea butterfly as seen under a microscope

Sea Angel

| LATIN NAME: *Clione limacina* | SIZE: 2 INCHES/5 CENTIMETERS |
A QUICK-SWIMMING PREDATORY SEA SLUG

The stunning, delicate-looking sea angel is actually a ruthless deadly hunter, and its preferred prey is the sea butterfly. After a frenzied chase, it grasps the sea butterfly with its tentacle-like arms, then uses the sharp hooks in its mouth to pull the sea butterfly's soft body from its shell before swallowing it whole.

Sea angels beat their "wings" in a rowing motion, about twice a minute when at rest.

They don't have eyes but use chemical senses to detect prey. When one senses a victim, it moves fast.

Sea angels are themselves preyed upon by fish and planktonic feeders, such as baleen whales.

A sea angel hunting a sea butterfly

Moon Jelly

| Latin name: *Aurelia aurita* | Size: adults up to 15 inches/38 centimeters |
Jellies are invertebrates with a body shaped like a bell and trailing tentacles.

Jellies go through four very different stages before reaching their adult form. The final phase before adulthood is the ephyra larval phase, during which the baby jellies are not even ½ inch/1.25 centimeters wide. These newly budded jellies look like snowflakes and gently pulsate as they drift on the currents, pulling in even smaller plankton to feed on. It takes ephyrae a few months to achieve their adult size.

A jelly's life begins with a fertilized egg, which develops into a planula, a free-swimming larva.

The planula attaches to a firm surface, where it transforms into a flower-like polyp, with a mouth and tentacles.

The polyp forms stacks of tiny ephyrae, which break off and swim away. The ephyrae then develop into adult jellies.

Moon jelly ephyra larvae as seen under a microscope

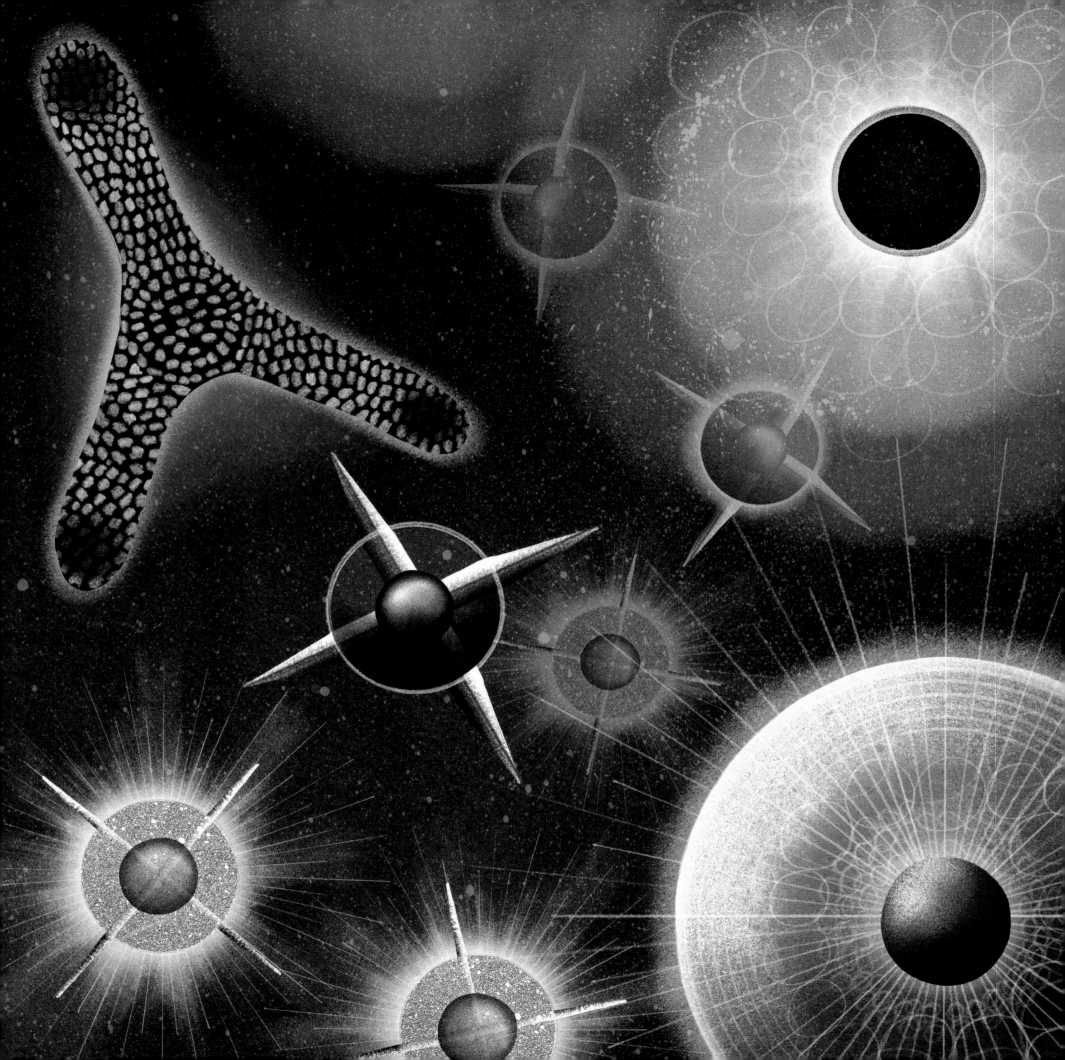

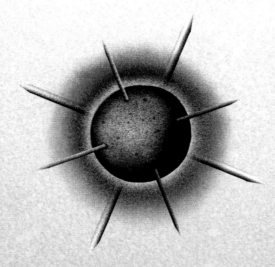

Radiolaria

| SIZE: 30 MICROMETERS–$^1/_{16}$ INCH/2 MILLIMETERS |
A GROUP OF SINGLE-CELLED ORGANISMS WITH COMPLEX SILICA SKELETONS

Radiolaria are a type of zooplankton, and can be found drifting in oceans all over the world. Their skeletons are made of a mineral called silica and have a sturdy crystal structure that radiates from a central point. Because of their strong silica structures, radiolaria skeletons have been well preserved in the fossil record over hundreds of millions of years. There have been thousands of species, both fossil and living, each with its own unique structure.

Many radiolaria species are only hundredths of millimeters long, but some are visible to the human eye.

They feed on passing bacteria or plankton, including diatoms and copepods.

They capture their food using long needle-like "pseudopods," which extend from their cell membrane.

Radiolaria as seen under a microscope

Acantharea

| SIZE: 30 MICROMETERS–$^1/_{16}$ INCH/2 MILLIMETERS |
SINGLE-CELLED ORGANISMS RELATED TO RADIOLARIA

With their elaborate mineral skeletons, acantharea are some of the most beautiful of all plankton. On calm days, they drift toward the surface layers of the open ocean, soaking up the sunlight. Like coral, many species have a symbiotic relationship with microalgae. The acantharea provide nutrients and a safe home, while the microalgae capture energy from the sun.

Acantharea as seen under a microscope

Acantharea skeletons consist of
rod-like spines called spicules.
Unlike radiolarians', their skeletons
do not fossilize, so acantharea
are never preserved.

The arrangement of the spines in
their skeletons is incredibly precise.
They grow out from the center and
are uniformly spaced.

Into the Deep

Hidden deep beneath the ocean waves lies a
world where strange creatures thrive. It is a
world rarely seen by human eyes, yet it is home
to an extraordinary variety of life. Fearsome
anglerfish hang in the water with gaping fanged
jaws, bioluminescent jellies and shrimp flicker
like neon signs in the darkness, and ghostly
white crabs gather by the thousands
around volcanic sea vents.

Giant Pacific Octopus

| LATIN NAME: *ENTEROCTOPUS DOFLEINI* | SIZE: 16 FEET/5 METERS |
A HUGE CEPHALOPOD WITH A SOFT BODY AND A POWERFUL BEAK

Swaying in the ocean current, a clutch of giant Pacific octopus eggs lies hidden inside a rocky outcrop. From the moment the eggs are laid through the months it takes them to hatch, the female octopus guards over them, rarely leaving the den and never eating. When the hatchlings finally emerge, they are less than a $1/4$ inch/6 millimeters long. The mother's role as protector takes everything out of her, and shortly after her eggs have hatched, she dies, starving and exhausted.

In some species, the eggs can take over four years to hatch. The mother watches over them throughout.

The giant Pacific octopus is one of the largest species of octopus, with an arm span of more than 13 feet/4 meters.

This colossal octopus appears in ancient legends and is said to be capable of ripping a ship in two.

Close-up view of giant Pacific octopus hatchling and eggs

Swordtail Squid

| LATIN NAME: *CHIROTEUTHIS CALYX* | SIZE: 12 INCHES/30 CENTIMETERS |
A CEPHALOPOD WITH EIGHT ARMS ARRANGED IN PAIRS AND TWO, USUALLY LONGER, TENTACLES

In the deep waters of the North Pacific, a swordtail squid lies patiently
in wait, motionless in the dark. Its translucent body allows it to keep out
of sight while its enormous eyes help it to spy its prey. On the tips of its
tentacles are glowing lures that mimic smaller bioluminescent creatures.
A passing shrimp might be enticed by the promise of food and will find
it is dinner instead.

In a world of near darkness,
many deep-sea creatures
use bioluminescence to
create their own light.

Bioluminescence can be
used to entice prey, attract a
mate, scare off predators, or
mimic other creatures.

When startled, the
swordtail squid escapes,
leaving a jet of ink that
resembles its body shape.

A shrimp being lured by a swordtail
squid's bioluminescent tentacles

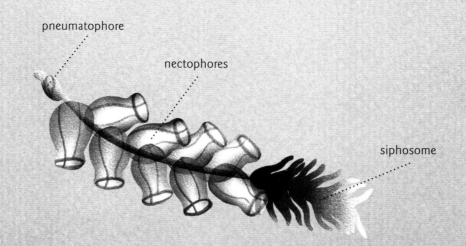

pneumatophore

nectophores

siphosome

Deep-Sea Siphonophore

| LATIN NAME: *MARRUS ORTHOCANNA* | SIZE: 7 FEET/2 METERS |
A SIPHONOPHORE IS A COLONY OF INDIVIDUAL ANIMALS LINKED TOGETHER BY A LONG STEM.

A *Marrus orthocanna* wends slowly through the cold, deep Arctic Ocean like a great chain of Chinese lanterns. Every now and then it pauses, then puts out its "fishing lines" to ensnare passing animals. But this is not a single creature. It is a colony of individual animals working together. Each member of this community has its special role. Some catch prey; others digest food. Some reproduce, while others do the swimming.

Marrus orthocanna is topped by an orange gas-filled pneumatophore, which keeps the colony afloat.

Just below that are jar-shaped nectophores, which propel the colony forward, backward, and sideways.

Trailing behind is its siphosome, responsible for catching prey, reproduction, and other vital tasks.

A siphonophore snaring a fish with its sticky tentacles

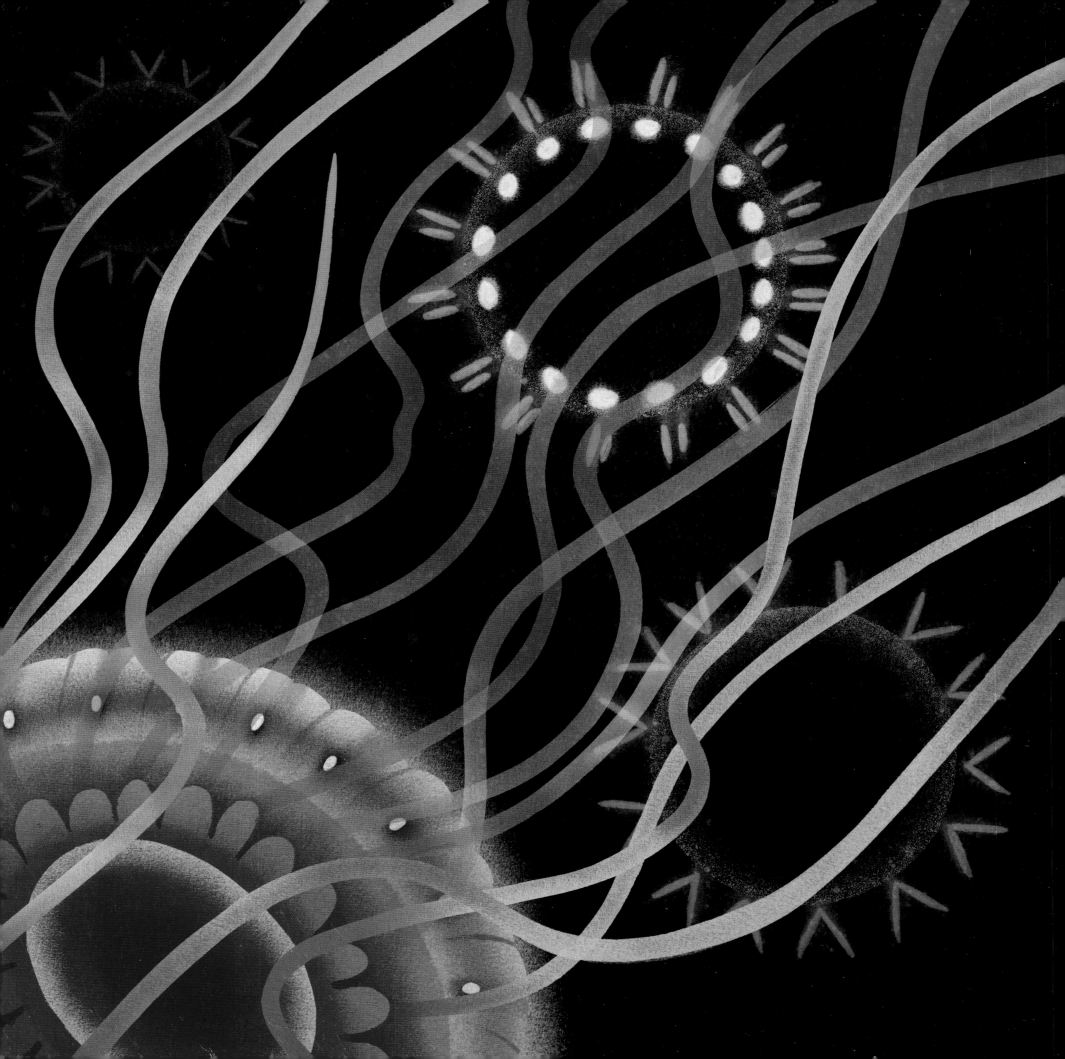

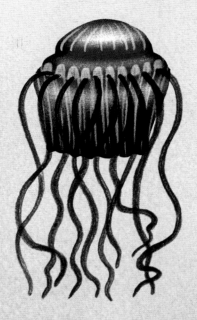

Atolla Jelly

| Latin name: *Atolla wyvillei* | Size: 6–8 inches/15–20 centimeters in diameter |
A deep-sea species of crown jelly

Gliding like a spaceship through the deep, the atolla jelly has an extraordinary
way of escaping harm. When threatened by a predator, it lets off a spiraling
display of flashing blue lights. This bioluminescent light show acts like a
burglar alarm, which draws in a larger animal to come and eat its attacker
while the atolla swims away to safety.

The atolla lives in depths of
3,300–13,000 feet/1,000–
4,000 meters in a region
known as the midnight zone.

The deep-red atolla may look
colorful to our eyes, but red
is one of the first colors to
become invisible at depth.

The fact that the atolla's red
coloring becomes invisible in deep
water helps it to hide from predators
and catch its prey.

Atolla jellies displaying
their bioluminescence

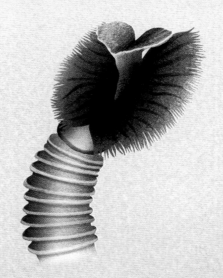

Giant Tube Worms

| LATIN NAME: *RIFTIA PACHYPTILA* | SIZE: UP TO 8 FEET/2 METERS LONG |
MARINE INVERTEBRATES WITH TUBULAR BODIES

Along the deep ocean floor, colossal hydrothermal vents spew clouds of toxic fluids that are hot enough to melt lead. At depths of around 6,000 feet/1,800 meters, the pressure is immense and there is no sunlight, yet life thrives around the vents — including bustling communities of mussels, fish, lobsters, white crabs, anemones, and, towering above them all, giant red-tipped tube worms.

Life is possible at these depths because of the trillions of single-celled bacteria and organisms at the bottom of the food chain.

These organisms convert the mineral-rich fluids from the vents into energy through a process called chemosynthesis.

Life at these depths has been discovered only recently. Until the late 1970s, scientists thought the deep seabed was largely barren.

Giant tube worms and mussels clinging to a deep-sea vent

Radiolarian Ooze

| SIZE: 30 MICROMETERS–$^1/_{16}$ INCH/2 MILLIMETERS |
THE SKELETAL REMAINS OF RADIOLARIANS THAT SETTLE ON THE OCEAN FLOOR

Near the ocean floor, a steady shower of dead plankton rains slowly down. Some particles will float for weeks before finally reaching the bottom. Among them are the delicate microscopic shells and skeletons of radiolarians.

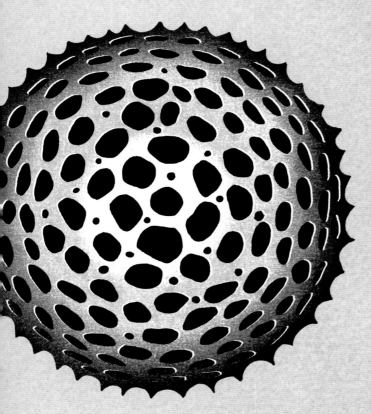

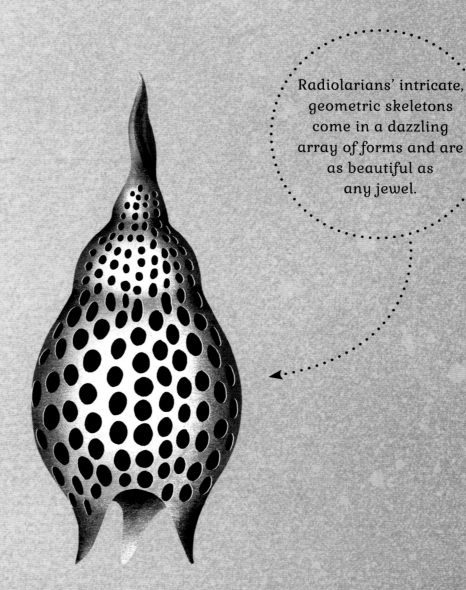

Radiolarians' intricate, geometric skeletons come in a dazzling array of forms and are as beautiful as any jewel.

Ever since radiolarians were discovered, they have inspired scientists, architects, painters, and sculptors.

Microscopic radiolarian skeletons found in deep-sea sediments

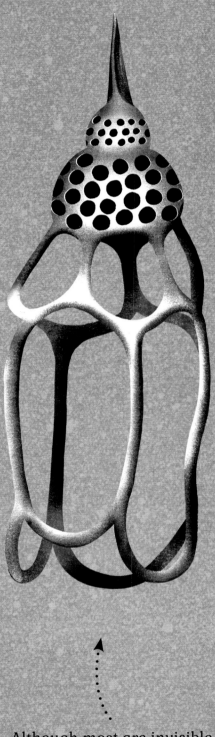

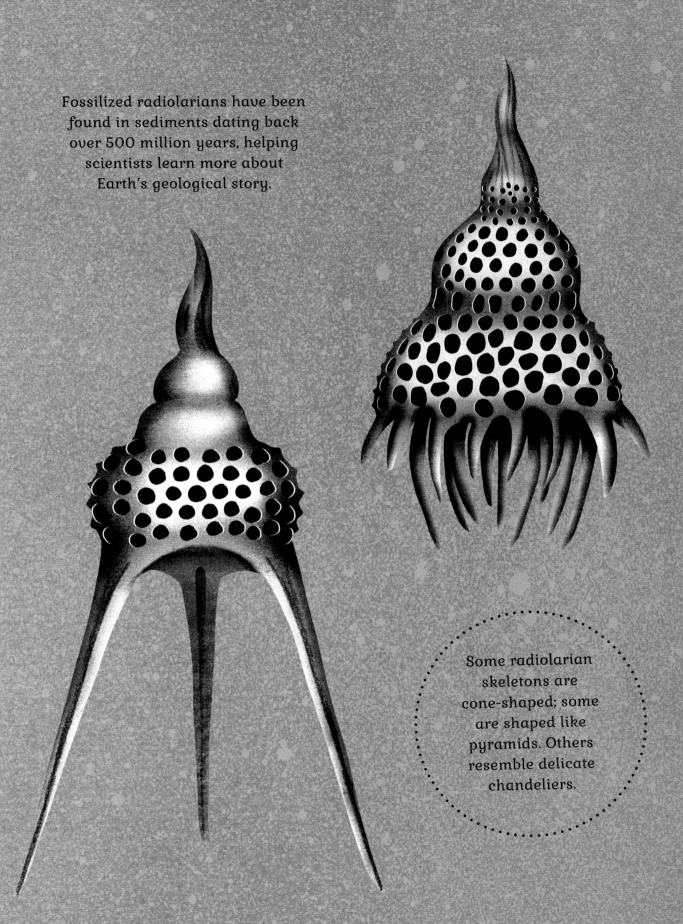

Fossilized radiolarians have been found in sediments dating back over 500 million years, helping scientists learn more about Earth's geological story.

Although most are invisible to the naked eye, radiolarian skeletons are amazingly complex.

Some radiolarian skeletons are cone-shaped; some are shaped like pyramids. Others resemble delicate chandeliers.

Selected Bibliography

Published Works

Dipper, Frances. *The Marine World: A Natural History of Ocean Life*. Plymouth, England: Wild Nature, 2016.

Haeckel, Ernst. *Art Forms from the Ocean: The Radiolarian Prints of Ernst Haeckel*. New York: Prestel, 2005.

———. *Art Forms in Nature*. New York: Dover Publications, 1974.

Hoyt, Erich. *Creatures of the Deep: In Search of the Sea's Monsters and the World They Live In*. Buffalo, NY: Firefly, 2014.

Kirby, Richard R. *Ocean Drifters: A Secret World Beneath the Waves*. Buffalo, NY: Firefly, 2011.

Knowlton, Nancy. *Citizens of the Sea: Wondrous Creatures from the Census of Marine Life*. Washington, DC: National Geographic Society, 2010.

MacQuitty, Miranda. *Ocean*. New York: Dorling Kindersley, 2014.

Sardet, Christian. *Plankton: Wonders of the Drifting World*. Chicago: University of Chicago Press, 2015.

Online Sources

Monterey Bay Aquarium
https://www.montereybayaquarium.org/

National Fish and Wildlife Foundation
http://www.nfwf.org/coralreef/Pages/home.aspx

National Geographic
http://www.nationalgeographic.com/environment/oceans/

National Oceanic and Atmospheric Administration (NOAA)
http://www.noaa.gov
http://oceanservice.noaa.gov

National Oceanography Centre
http://noc.ac.uk/

Oceana
http://oceana.org/marine-life/corals-and-other-invertebrates

Plankton Chronicles
http://planktonchronicles.org/

Siphonophores.org
http://www.siphonophores.org

Smithsonian Ocean Portal
http://ocean.si.edu

Tree of Life Web Project
http://tolweb.org/

World Register of Marine Species
http://www.marinespecies.org/

World Wildlife Organization
http://www.worldwildlife.org/habitats/ocean-habitat

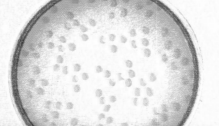

The author, illustrator, and publisher would like to thank Adam Waugh, Technical Specialist at the U.K. Environment Agency, for his expert review of this book.

No matter how far we live from the shore, the ocean affects all our lives. Not only does it support an astonishing diversity of life — much of which has yet to be discovered — but it also provides the water we drink, the food we eat, and the very air we breathe. Yet this precious ecosystem is increasingly under threat from pollution, overfishing, and rising sea temperatures. Uncover more ocean secrets and find out how you can help to protect marine wildlife and habitats across the world by visiting these websites:

Census of Marine Life
http://www.coml.org

National Geographic
http://ocean.nationalgeographic.com/environment/oceans/

National Oceanic and Atmospheric Administration (NOAA)
http://www.noaa.gov

Oceana
http://oceana.org

Plankton Chronicles
http://planktonchronicles.org/

Sea Life Trust
https://www.sealifetrust.org